FOCUS ON THE FAMILY®

20 BIBLE STORIES
Every Child Should Know
with 20 original Bible memory songs on full-length CD

songs by Little Man Music

Standard Publishing
cincinnati, ohio

Heritage Builders®

Acknowledgements
Contributing story and activity writers: Geri Benter, Carrie Girton, Kathy Grove, Kerry Kloth, Adrienne Miklovic, Tammy Nischan, Vivian Reed, Kim Seevers, Robin Stanley, Gary Thacker, Elisha Walker.

Contributing illustrators: Dan Foote, Michael Streff, Christine Tripp (cover and interior).

Songwriters: Scott Liebenow (It Is Good; Rain, Rain, Rain; God Keeps His Promises; The Ten Commandments; You'll Never Believe; Just Have Faith; This Time I'll Do What You Say; Birth of Jesus; What Are Friends For?; Storms; The News; Don't Shoo Them Away; Alive!; Dynamic Duo); Cathy Liebenow (The Ten Commandments; This Time I'll Do What You Say; And There Were 10; Alive!); Scott Graffius (God's Ways Are the Best; It Pays to Be Kind; No Matter What the Cost; A Friend Indeed; Zacchaeus).

CD recorded, mixed, and mastered by Glen West at Gap Digital, Wheaton, Illinois. Additional recording by Scott Allen at Eagle Mountain Recording Studios, Newark, Texas.

Singers: Rebekah Kinsman, Cathy Liebenow, Cassandra Peletis, Catherine Willms.

Soloists: Richard Liebenow and Rebekah Kinsman (The Ten Commandments), Beth Maas (Just Have Faith), Cassandra Peletis and Nathan Gregory (Storms), Joy Curry and Sarah Hammons (Alive!).

Musicians: Scott Liebenow (keyboards, drums, programming); Errol Brown (bass); Scott Graffius (guitar).

ISBN 0-7847-1586-6

10 09 08 07 06 05 04   9 8 7 6 5 4 3 2 1

20 Bible Stories Every Child Should Know

Table of Contents

New Testament

A NOTE TO PARENTS

Have you been looking for a fun, new resource to help your children learn Bible stories? Well, you've found it—and more! *20 Bible Stories Every Child Should Know* has fun-to-sing music, read-aloud stories, and simple-to-do activities that will inspire and challenge.

The 20 stories in this book have been chosen to represent basic Bible concepts that should be a part of every child's life. They will strengthen your child's spiritual journey by encouraging him to know and serve the God he loves.

For every Bible story you will find:

— A brand-new song on the full-length stereo CD that tells the Bible story. Everyone in your family will enjoy the wonderful variety of music that has been especially written and recorded just for this project!

— Full lyrics for the Bible story song to help you sing along with the CD. They make it easy to join your child in the fun of learning the story set to music.

— A contemporary story that relates the theme of the Bible story to everyday life. Read it together and allow it to spark conversations with your child about his own similar experiences. (Don't forget to share *your* own stories too!)

— Two story boosters that suggest simple activities for recalling and understanding the Bible story. Use them to create teachable moments as you guide your child toward making God's Word a natural part of life.

If your family enjoyed learning Bible stories with this book, get the companion *20 Bible Verses Every Child Should Know* and discover the fun of learning Bible verses set to music!

IT IS GOOD

Day 1—God created light
Day 2—He created the sky
Day 3—God created
The oceans, flowers, and trees

And He said it is good, it is good, it is good
What I created is good
It is good, it is good, it is good, so good

Day 4—He made the moon, the stars, the sun
Day 5—He made the birds and the fish
Day 6—the people and the animals
Day 7—God rested!

And He said it is good, it is good, it is good
What I created is good
It is good, it is good, it is good, so good

THE WORLD GOD MADE

One fall day, Daddy and Brooke went outside to rake all the colorful leaves in the yard. Daddy's job was raking; Brooke's job was rolling on the leaves to be sure none got away.

"Daddy, our Sunday school teacher told us that God made the world. Did you know that?" Brooke asked.

"Yes, I did," Daddy answered. "While you're keeping those leaves from blowing around, why don't you tell me about the things you see that God made."

"I see light!" Brooke said excitedly. "It's just like on the first day when God made light. He called the light day and the darkness night."

"Now look up. What do you see?" asked Daddy.

Brooke looked up and saw the sky. "God made the sky on the second day."

"Why don't we take a break from all this leaf-raking," Daddy said as he took Brooke's hand and walked toward the pond behind their house. "When God made the world, at first it was all water. But on the third day He made all the land," Daddy told Brooke.

"Our Sunday school teacher said He also made the pretty flowers and plants," said Brooke. "He even made the trees and all the different colors of leaves—red, green, brown, orange, and yellow. The yellow ones are my favorite!"

Brooke and Daddy looked up at the sky. The sun was going down and the stars were beginning to shine. "Daddy, this is like the fourth day when God made the sun, moon, and stars."

Soon Daddy and Brooke gathered up the rakes and headed toward the house. Brooke looked around one last time before they went through the door. "Daddy," she said. "I'm glad God made so many beautiful things to see." She was glad He made daddies too.

Genesis 1:1 says, "In the beginning God created the heavens and the earth." God gave us a beautiful world to live in and to take care of. While Brooke and her daddy were taking care of their yard, they remembered that God made all the beautiful things around them. What do you see around you that God made? Remember to think about God when you look around at His beautiful world. Thank Him for making it!

STORY BOOSTERS

★ Make a poster that says at the top: God made everything and everything God made is good. Have everyone in your family cut and paste a picture of one of their favorite things God made. Remember to thank God for those things when you have family prayer time.

★ The next time your family takes a trip, help your child take pictures of various things you see that God made. When you return home, gather the pictures into a scrapbook. Enjoy coming up with fun captions together that celebrate God and His wonderful creations!

RAIN, RAIN, RAIN

God was looking at His people one day
He was unhappy with the choices they'd made
So God said to Noah I'm gonna start new
Well except for you

God told Noah to build a big boat
And his neighbors said hey you that won't float
And even if it looked very odd, Noah obeyed God
But he was probably thinkin'

Rain, rain, rain—did You say that it is gonna
Rain, rain, rain—You're gonna flood the earth
Rain rain, rain—everyone will be gone except me
I will be so lonely

The ark was very full, did you know
That God had asked him to bring some cargo
You can bring your wife and you can bring your boys
There's one more thing I hope you don't mind noise
Two of every animal will be just fine; Noah didn't whine
But he was probably thinkin'

Rain, rain, rain—go away come back another day
Rain, rain, rain—this flood is getting higher
Rain, rain, rain—so much rain I can't even see
There's a giraffe in front of me

For 40 days and nights he rode through the storm
The ark was keeping all the animals warm
Noah sent a dove to find some dry land
Forty days and nights were all Noah could stand
Then the bird came back, out came the sun
The flood was finally done

And Noah was saying
Rain, rain, rain—thank You God for sending it away
Rain, rain, rain—this flood is finally over
Rain, rain, rain—thank You God for all Your power
And this 40-day shower

17

OBEY WHEN IT'S HARD

Mom told Avery not to go outside. "It has been raining all day and it will be very muddy," she said. "Please do not go out."

When Mom left the room, Avery's cousin Ben said, "Let's just stand on the porch. There is no mud on the porch."

"But the porch is still outside and Mom said not to go outside," said Avery.

Ben wanted to go outside! He thought it was just plain silly that Avery wouldn't even go out as far as the porch.

"Come on," he whined. "Your mom will never know!"

Avery was sad that Ben wanted to ignore what his mom had told them. Although Avery didn't want his cousin to be upset, he knew that it was important to obey his mom.

Later, Avery told his mom that Ben tried to talk him into going outside to play on the porch, even after she had told them not to. But Mom didn't get angry. Instead, she told Avery how proud she was that he made the right choice. "Sometimes it does seem hard to obey," she said as she gave him a big hug. "And sometimes we have to help others make right choices too."

Avery was glad he chose to obey his mom. Even though he wanted to play outside, it felt good to do the right thing.

Obeying his mom was hard for Avery because he was the only one who wanted to do the right thing. In the Bible story, God asked Noah to do some things that would have seemed pretty crazy. What were they? What did Noah do, even though it was hard to do? He obeyed! Think about a time when you chose to do the right thing even when it was hard.

STORY BOOSTERS

★ To help you remember one way that Noah obeyed, look around your house and find things that come in pairs. As you look at your collection of pairs, recall the ways that Noah obeyed God.

★ As you sing about Noah, do motions to help remember key parts of the story. For example, when you sing "rain, rain, rain," clap your hands rapidly on your legs. And for "build a big boat," make hammering motions.

GOD KEEPS HIS PROMISES

Abraham was an old, old man going on 100 years old
He had a wife and her name was Sarah; she had a heart of gold
One day God said to Abraham, I have a blessing for you
Your wife Sarah is gonna have a baby and give a son to you
(spoken) So Abraham waited and waited and waited

God said, look do you see those stars? There are so many up there
Your family's gonna be that big but Abraham said, where is my heir
Sarah and I have been waiting a long time for this
God said don't worry; what is your hurry
I keep my promises

Chorus:
God keeps His promises (repeat)
Even when it seems like He will not

Abraham said, well this is real nice but have you seen us lately
We stopped thinking about having children after we turned 80
Sarah agreed with Abraham; she said, I'm too old for this
God said you will see; I will bless your family
I keep my promises

Isaac was born the very next year just like God had told them
Abraham and Sarah jumped for joy; they were blessed
    to have him
Everyone will rejoice with us as soon as they hear this
Now you can see from this great story that
God keeps His promises

(Repeat chorus twice)

HELPING OUT

Hope's mother was very ill. Dad explained to Hope and her sister that their mother was going to be taking some medicine that would make her very tired.

"You girls will need to do some things for yourselves until your mom starts to feel better," their dad said. "You can get the table ready for breakfast, make your sandwiches for lunch, fix your hair, and clean up after yourselves."

Both Hope and her sister nodded their heads. They promised to work together to help out around the house however they could.

The two sisters worked very hard. They got up early the next day. Before they left for school, they picked out their clothes, had cereal and toast, put their dishes in the dishwasher, and made their beds.

And when they arrived home, Hope and her sister helped Dad with supper. Hope set the table while her sister stirred the macaroni and cheese and poured them some milk. They even did their homework without complaining!

At the end of the day when they went in to kiss their mom goodnight, she hugged them and said, "Thank you for helping out so much around the house. I feel better just knowing that you girls are keeping your promise to your dad. I'll be up and around soon. Then I can be the one to help YOU around the house!"

Just then Dad peeked around the corner and winked at them. He blew their mom a kiss before leaning down to kiss the girls on their foreheads. Hope and her sister were happy to keep their promise to help out.

Hope and her sister made a promise to their dad and they kept their promise. Sometimes promises are hard for us to keep. But in the Bible story about Abraham, we read about someone who ALWAYS keeps His promises—God! He promised Abraham and his wife Sarah a son. "And the Lord did . . . what he had promised" (Genesis 21:1). Do you know what they named the baby God gave them? Isaac!

STORY BOOSTERS

★ Brainstorm with your child to discover several of God's promises. Write each one on a card and put the cards in a box. Each night at dinner pick a promise and talk about ways God keeps His promises. Then pray and thank God for His promise.

★ Help your child make a book of his own promises. Cut a stack of paper all the same size. Punch holes through which you will tie a piece of yarn. On each page, have your child write something he promises to do. For example, feed the dog or take out the garbage.

GOD'S WAYS ARE THE BEST

Joseph was a man with brothers who were mean
They threw him down into the biggest hole you've ever seen
Filled with jealousy they sent him far away
But little did they know that they would need his help someday

Chorus:
Sometimes it's not easy to know just what to do
The Bible has the answers; you know God's Word is true
In Genesis we read how Joseph passed the test
He forgave his brothers 'cause God's ways are the best

Many years had passed and God was helping Joe
To save the land of Egypt when their food supply was low
Then his brothers came not knowing he was there
They needed to buy food because at home it was so rare

(Repeat chorus)

Joseph loved the Lord and in his faith he grew
And when his brothers came he knew exactly what to do
God can take the bad and turn it into good
Joseph loved his brothers and forgave them like he should

(Repeat chorus)

Now whose ways are the best? God's ways!
And when are they best? Always!
And what about the rest? No way!
God knows best!
That's right!

(Repeat chorus)

BACKYARD PLAYTIME

"Matthew, please play with your brother in the backyard," Mom asked as she began to cook dinner.

"But, Mom, my friends are all out playing kickball. I want to play with them!" Matthew answered.

"Now, Matthew, you can play with your friends anytime," his mom said. "I need your help right now."

Matthew took Jon with him to the backyard. His friends were playing next door. *I have a great idea,* Matthew said to himself. *I will make Jon sit in the grass and watch us play.*

Jon grew very hot and lonely sitting in the grass, but Matthew ignored him and had fun with his friends. He didn't even let his brother grab the ball that came his way by accident.

That evening at dinner, Mom said, "So, Jon, did you have a nice time with your brother?" Jon just looked at Matthew. He knew his brother would be in big trouble if he told his mom about what happened.

But Matthew spoke up, "No, Jon did not have fun. I made him sit in the grass while I played kickball. I didn't want him to bother us. I'm sorry, Mom."

"I think you need to tell someone else you are sorry," said Mom.

Matthew turned to Jon and said, "I'm sorry, Jon. Will you forgive me?"

"Yes, I forgive you," said Jon.

"Thanks!" said Matthew. "Tomorrow when we go outside, we'll play whatever game YOU want to play!"

What did Jon do even though his brother wasn't very nice to him? He forgave him! The Bible story about Joseph tells about a time when his brothers were mean to him. But what did Joseph do when his brothers needed help? He said, "I will provide for you" (Genesis 45:11), and he forgave them. The next time someone does something to you that isn't so nice, what will you do?

STORY BOOSTERS

★ Use these words from the Joseph song as a fun chant to help your child remember to make good choices when it comes to forgiveness: "Whose ways are the best? God's ways! And when are they the best? Always!"

★ Hide a cup in the room and have your child find it. As she searches, tell her what Joseph did to reveal himself to his brothers. Also talk about how his brothers may have felt when he forgave them.

THE TEN COMMANDMENTS

Moses led the Hebrews out of Egypt
By God's grace escaped a life of slavery
They were on their way to a better place
Where they could be safe and free

Then the Hebrews started to complain
They said, where is this so-called promised land
And so Moses went up a mountain and prayed
God, these folks are getting out of hand
And God replied with these commands

One—I am the only God you can worship
Two—you cannot worship idols or other things
Three—you cannot use my name in a bad way
Four—the Sabbath is a holy day
Five—you must honor your mother and father
Six—and you must not kill
Seven—you must stay faithful to your mate
Eight—and never steal from anyone
Nine—never ever tell a lie
Ten—do not want what your neighbor has
These are the Ten Commandments

(Repeat commandments)

A VERY SMART CHOICE

It was Sarah's birthday! Sarah got a bouncy little puppy as a birthday present from her parents. She was so excited she could hardly wait to go play with him! Sarah got a bunch of other cool presents from her friends too. She was going to have fun playing with her new toys and her new puppy.

As they were cleaning up from the birthday party, Sarah's mom said to her, "Sarah, puppies are fun, but taking care of them is hard work sometimes. There are some rules you are going to need to follow, but we know you can do it. Puppies need lots of food, water, and attention. So, it's going to be your job to give those things to him every day. You also need to play with your puppy outside."

"OK, Mom," said Sarah. She filled the puppy's bowls with food and water. Then she put the puppy in the backyard and went upstairs to her room. Sarah wanted to play with her new toys.

After a few minutes, she heard her puppy outside. He was barking. She kept playing with her toys. The puppy kept barking. Sarah thought about what her mom had said about taking care of the puppy. She didn't want to stop playing with her toys, but Sarah knew she should obey her mom.

When Sarah walked downstairs, the puppy was sitting by the back door with a stick in his mouth. Sarah smiled. Her puppy was waiting for her to come and play fetch! Sarah had fun playing with her puppy and she was glad she had obeyed.

Exodus 20:12 says, "Honor your father and your mother." It's one of the Ten Commandments God gave to Moses for His people. Sarah honored her mother because she obeyed. What are some of the other Commandments God wants us to obey?

STORY BOOSTERS

★ Make a rules magnet to remind your family to follow God's rules. Cut stone tablet shapes from a card. Help your child write some of God's rules on it in his own words. Glue a piece of magnet on the back and hang it on the fridge.

★ Play the classic game Rock, Paper, Scissors with your family. Choose a leader before beginning. The person whose motion matches the leader's choice names a rule. Discuss the rule, why God gave us the rule, and how to obey it.

YOU'LL NEVER BELIEVE

Here we are; we're going to the promised land
We are tired; our shoes are full of sand
We arrived at this place called Jericho
And you'll never believe what God has told us, never
You'll never believe what God has told us to do

God told us to march around the wall
Do this and the wall is sure to fall
It sounds so funny; this just can't be right
But we're marching around this great big city, marching
We're marching around the city of Jericho

Joshua is our leader
God shows him where to go
Life will be much sweeter
When we get through Jericho

'Round and 'round we march 'round Jericho
We started marching seven days ago
There is only one more thing to do
And you'll never believe what God has told us, never
You'll never believe what God has told us to do

He told us to yell—AHHHHHHHHHHHHH
And blow our horns

Rumble, rumble, rumble, the walls came rumbling down
Crumble, crumble, crumble, the walls came
    crumbling down
Tumble, tumble, tumble, the walls came tumbling down
AHHHHHHHHHHHHHH

JIMMY TRIES AGAIN

As Mom hung towels on the clothesline, she saw Jimmy walking home from Jake's house. She wondered why he was shuffling his feet and moving so slowly.

"Jimmy, why do you look so sad?" she asked him.

"I can't play catch as well as Jake does," he said. "I dropped the ball and Jake laughed at me."

"Don't worry, Jimmy," Mom said as she hugged him tight. "You will get better with practice. Just keep trying!"

Tears rolled down Jimmy's sad face. "I don't want to try!" he cried. "I'll never get better at playing catch!"

Mom wiped away his tears and said, "Jimmy, do you remember the Bible story about Joshua?"

Jimmy thought for a second. "Yes, I remember," he said.

Mom went on, "God asked Joshua to do some things that Joshua was not sure he could do. But do you know what Joshua did? He did his best and God helped him."

"Do you think God can help me be brave like Joshua?" he asked.

"Yes," replied Mom. "God loves to help all of us do our best."

Jimmy got excited. He couldn't wait to start practicing. "Can I go to Jake's tomorrow?" he asked. "I want to try playing catch again!"

Mom gave Jimmy a hug. "That is a super idea," she said.

Jimmy learned an important lesson from the Bible—God will help us do the things we can't do on our own. Joshua 6:27 says that God was with Joshua. That means God was always there to help Joshua. God is with you, too, and he wants to help you. What are some ways that God can help you to be brave?

STORY BOOSTERS

★ As you sing the song about Joshua, see how many actions your child can come up with. Then do them all together—no snoozing!

★ Pray together using "popcorn praises." Each person says a quick sentence to praise God for His might and power. Before praying, brainstorm a list of ways God shows His power.

IT PAYS TO BE KIND

Long ago there was a widow named Ruth
Naomi was her mother-in-law
Ruth said don't worry I will take care of you
I will be there and together we will live for the Lord

Chorus:
It pays to be kind to somebody in need
Spreading God's love to each person I see
Helping the world by sharing the truth
I can be kind like Ruth

Every day I have so much to do
It's easy to forget to show God's love to the world
God is faithful and He always provides
Just like Naomi and Ruth I will live for the Lord

(Repeat chorus)

God had something special planned for Ruth
A chance to find a love of her own
Then she met Boaz a man from nearby
They fell in love and got married
And they lived for the Lord

(Repeat chorus twice)

37

FOLLOW THE LEADER

Monday morning came, and Claire rode the bus to school as she did every day. Spelling was her first class for the day. Next would come math and science. Once science was over, recess would be just around the corner. Claire hoped recess would come quickly.

Brrrrrriiinnnggg. At last, the bell for recess! Mrs. Oliver led them to the playground where Claire and her friends jumped rope. While they were playing, a new girl asked to join them. Her name was Tracy. She had moved into town right before Christmas. Claire liked her. But her friends did not want to jump rope with Tracy. Tracy started to walk away.

This upset Claire. She wanted to please her friends, but she wanted to make a new friend too. Claire thought about what to do. "Wait!" she finally called. Tracy turned around. "How about a game of catch?" Claire asked.

"I love playing catch," Tracy said with a smile. The two new friends had a great time playing together. Tracy was thankful for Claire's kindness. She usually just sat by herself during recess.

Soon the bell rang and recess was over. Claire's friends walked toward her and Tracy. She was afraid they were coming over to make fun of her. But one friend said to Tracy, "Maybe tomorrow we can all play together!" Claire was happy that she had chosen to be kind to Tracy, even though it was hard to stand up to her friends. She knew she had made the right decision to be kind. Now Tracy will have many new friends to play with at recess.

The Bible tells about a woman named Ruth who was kind even when it was hard. She went to live with Naomi in a strange place and helped her by gathering grain from nearby fields for bread. Let's think of some ways that we can "be kind like Ruth" to the people around us.

STORY BOOSTERS

★ Put several items into a paper bag— bandage, toy, paper plates, markers, can of food, quarter, dishcloth, etc. Pull out an item and tell a way that it can be used to show kindness to others. Act out what that kindness would look like.

★ As a family, read the story of Ruth. Then choose a way your family can be kind to someone in your neighborhood. Maybe you can clean up someone's yard!

JUST HAVE FAITH

David was a little guy it says in Samuel's book
He relied on the Lord; he was stronger than he looked
Goliath was a giant man, the strongest Philistine
Nine feet tall, made a tree look small
He was nasty and real mean
He was shouting who will come and fight
David said, I'll beat you with God's might
The giant laughed out loud

Chorus:
It's amazing what God can do
He can use a child just like you
God will help you when you get scared
Just have faith; trust in God and He will be with you

David took his little sling and took five smooth rocks
As a shepherd boy he used his sling
To protect the sheep in his flock
He slung a rock and hit Goliath's head
With one shot the giant fell down dead
And the Philistines ran away

(Repeat chorus twice)

Just have faith like David did
And God will be with you

LILY

Lily sat in the dentist's chair. The dentist looked at her teeth with his special tools.

"Your teeth look great, Lily, except you have one tiny cavity," the dentist said. "I need to put a filling in that cavity before it gets worse."

The dentist talked to Lily's mom. Her mom made an appointment for them to come back to the dentist's office.

When they got home, Lily talked to her mom about how she felt. "I don't want the dentist to fill the cavity in my tooth," she said. "I am too afraid."

"I know you're afraid," her mom said. "Let's ask God to give you courage and help you not to be afraid."

Lily prayed, "Dear Jesus, help me to be brave. Please be with me when I get my cavity filled. Amen."

When Lily went to the dentist the next week, she felt only a little bit scared. She closed her eyes and prayed while the dentist worked on her tooth.

Before very long the dentist was finished, and Lily got to choose a prize from the colorful box on the counter. The dentist also gave her a new toothbrush.

Lily's tooth felt much better. She was glad she had prayed for courage. She knew that God would help her to be brave.

Lily knew that she could trust God to help her. The Bible tells about a boy who trusted God. His name was David. Because he knew God was on his side, David wasn't afraid to stand up to the giant soldier Goliath. He said, "The Lord . . . will deliver me" (1 Samuel 17:37). The next time you are afraid, whom will you trust to help you be brave?

STORY BOOSTERS

★ Gather some clean, smooth stones. Help your child write on one side of each of them, "Trust God." On the other side of each, write a situation in which your child needs to be like David and trust God to help her.

★ Visit a fire station and ask the men and women there what it means to be brave. Pray together with any who will allow you to. Thank God for them and their bravery and ask for His continued protection.

NO MATTER WHAT THE COST

Daniel was a servant of the king
But Daniel put God first in everything
There was a law that said no one could pray
But Daniel talked to God three times a day

Chorus:
I will pray to God for I know that He will listen
No matter what you say, I'm still gonna pray
Because without Him I'd be lost
I will pray to God no matter what the cost

The soldiers threw him down in the lions' den
But Daniel knew that God was a faithful friend
Daniel was protected by God's hand
And faith in God was spread throughout the land

(Repeat chorus)

When we pray God shows the way
And we find the strength to face the day
God will answer when we call
To help us through it all

(Repeat chorus)

AMELIA'S PRAYER

Amelia and her mom talked on the way home from church. "Amelia, I noticed you keep your eyes open when you pray at church. That's OK," said Mom, "but I was just wondering why you do it."

"I wait to pray until everyone else is done," said Amelia. "Then God can hear my prayer better."

Mom was surprised. "God can pay attention to everyone's prayers," she said.

"How can He do that?" asked Amelia. "I can't hear two people at once."

"God isn't like us," said Mom. "He is so powerful that He can hear everyone at once. In fact, God can do many things that we cannot do."

Amelia's eyes grew wide. She thought about her Sunday school class. "We learned in Sunday school that Daniel prayed to God. The king made him go into the place where the lions were. But God kept

Daniel safe from the hungry lions. We've been learning about a lot of things God can do."

"There are many stories of powerful things God has done. I'm glad God is so powerful," said Mom.

"Me too," said Amelia. "I'm going to pray and thank God for being so powerful."

"I'll pray too," said Mom.

"And He'll hear both of us!" Amelia said excitedly.

Daniel is a good example for us to follow. He loved God so much that he prayed even when the king said not to. Daniel knew that God was powerful enough to hear his prayer and to help him. The Bible says, "Three times a day he got down on his knees and prayed, giving thanks to his God, just as he had done before" (Daniel 6:10). Let's do what Amelia and her mom did—thank God for hearing our prayers and for being so powerful.

STORY BOOSTERS

★ Have your child place his hand on a piece of paper, fingers together. Trace his hand and cut it out. Write "pray to God" on the hand and use it as a reminder to pray like Daniel prayed.

★ As a family, go on a prayer walk in your house and in your neighborhood. Spend time thanking God for what you see—your room, a place to live, your neighbors—and asking Him to help you be a good example to the people you live with and near.

THIS TIME I'LL DO WHAT YOU SAY

There was a man whose name was Jonah
God told him to preach to the folks of Nineveh
It was a city so full of evil
Jonah decided not to go
And he got on a boat going the other way

While on the boat a storm was pounding
Jonah knew that God caused the storm
He told the sailors to throw him over
As soon as they did the storm stopped
And Jonah tried to swim away
But a huge fish swallowed him up

Chorus:
Jonah tried to run but it wasn't in God's plan
Jonah prayed to God to forgive that he was bad
He said I will never run away
This time I'll do what you say

Three days later God forgave Jonah
God told the fish to spit him out
Jonah was ready to go to Nineveh
To keep his promise and tell them about
God's mercy and forgiveness
They prayed and God forgave them

(Repeat chorus)

A SNEAKY SNACK

"Hi, Mom! I'm home," called Maria. Mom was in the kitchen. Maria gave her mom a hug. "May I please have a snack?" Maria asked. "I'm hungry."

"Sorry, Maria, not right now," Mom said. "Dad is coming home early tonight. If you eat something now, you won't be hungry for dinner."

Maria went to her room to play. Her stomach growled. She walked downstairs. When she saw that her mom wasn't in the kitchen, Maria got a box of crackers from the cabinet. She quickly ran to her room before her mom could see what she'd done.

Maria leaned against her bedroom door and grabbed a handful of crackers. As she chewed them, they seemed to stick in her mouth. She thought about what Mom had said. Maria felt bad. She opened her door and walked back to the kitchen.

"Mom, I took these crackers even though you said not to eat anything," said Maria as her eyes filled with tears. "I'm sorry."

Mom looked sad, but hugged Maria. "Thank you for telling me. I forgive you because you're sorry for what you did. Now, Maria, you need to ask God to forgive you. When you disobeyed me, you disobeyed Him."

"Will He forgive me too?" asked Maria.

"Of course He will," Mom said.

Maria learned about forgiveness from her mom. In the Bible story, Jonah learned about forgiveness when God sent a big fish to swallow him up! What did Jonah do while he was in the belly of that big fish? "Jonah prayed to the Lord" (Jonah 2:1) and asked Him for forgiveness. Then the Lord ordered the fish to spit up Jonah and it did. God forgave Jonah, and THIS time, Jonah obeyed and went to Nineveh!

STORY BOOSTERS

★ Throw blankets over a table or chairs to create an environment similar to the belly of the fish that swallowed Jonah. Gather your family into the space. Talk about what the belly may have been like and pretend to be Jonah asking God for forgiveness.

★ Practice together the forgiveness sentence: "I'm sorry; please forgive me." Talk about some scenarios that would require your child to make a right or a wrong choice. Then remind him of what to do when he makes a wrong choice.

BIRTH OF JESUS

Chorus:
We're here to tell you about the birth of Jesus
He's our Savior and Lord
We celebrate the miracle of God
The one we love and adore

Mary saw an angel (echo)
Joseph saw one too (echo)
He said don't worry Mary (echo)
I've got good news for you (echo)
You are going to give birth to God's Son
He is going to be the chosen one

(Repeat chorus)

Mary and her husband (echo)
They went to Bethlehem (echo)
The baby was a-comin' (echo)
But there were no rooms for them (echo)
Mary had the baby and Jesus was His name
In a lowly stable is how our Savior came

(Repeat chorus)

While shepherds watched their sheep at night
Unwinding and ready for bed
An angel told them of the Savior's birth
And this is what they said
This is a celebration (4 times)

(Repeat chorus twice)

CODY WORSHIPS JESUS

Cody's school class was getting ready for their big show. The children were going to sing songs for their family and friends.

"Does anyone want to sing a special song at the show?" the teacher asked.

None of the children raised their hands. They were afraid to sing alone in front of so many people.

But Cody raised his hand. "I want to sing a special song about Jesus," he said.

Some other children teased Cody because he wanted to sing a special song. But Cody didn't listen to them. Instead, he practiced every day so that his special song would be just right. Cody loved to sing songs and worship Jesus.

On the night of the show, Cody took a seat with his parents until his turn came. He had never seen so many people. Cody started to feel afraid. "Please, Jesus, help me to be brave and sing this song for You," Cody prayed.

When it was his turn to sing, Cody sang "Jesus Loves Me." He wasn't afraid anymore and he didn't forget any of the words.

When the song was over, everyone clapped. Cody felt happy. He was brave and sang a song to worship Jesus.

"Thank You, Jesus, for helping me sing a song for You," he prayed.

Cody sang a song for Jesus because Cody loves Jesus. When you do something to tell Jesus how much you love Him, it's called worship. When Jesus was born, many people came to worship Him. The Bible tells about shepherds who came from tending their flocks in the fields to worship baby Jesus. What did the shepherds do to worship Jesus? They ran to see Him. Then they ran to tell everyone about Him! How can you worship Jesus?

STORY BOOSTERS

★ Read together the account of Jesus' birth. Have your child try to imagine being able to visit baby Jesus. How would she have felt? What would she have done? What would YOU have done?

★ No matter what time of year it is, get out the Christmas music and sing together about the birth of Jesus. Remind your child that Jesus is God's Son and have a great time worshiping Him!

WHAT ARE FRIENDS FOR?

Jesus had 12 faithful men
Who went with Him everywhere
Preaching the Word and spreading good news
To everyone who was there

The faithful men were called disciples
Many were fishermen
Jesus called out come follow me and you will be fishers of men
And this is what they said

Chorus:
We'll follow You where You go
Sharing God's love with the people
You have called us to serve with You
So here we are what are friends for

They knew Jesus was God's Son
So they gave up everything
To learn from Him and share His love and to pray and sing
This is what they sang

(Repeat chorus)

And here are their names
Peter the rock, James and John, Andrew, Philip and Bartholomew
Matthew, Thomas and another James
Thaddeus, Simon and Judas Iscariot

We can be disciples too
Each and every day
All it takes is following Jesus
And here is what we should say

(Repeat chorus)

57

THE PARADE

Rat-a-tat-tat went the small drums. *Toot-toot-toot* went the shiny trumpets. Pete loved to see and hear the band. Grandpa and Pete liked to watch parades on television together.

"Oh, look, Grandpa!" shouted Pete. "There's the tuba!" *Oompa! Oompa!* went the big tuba.

"They are all walking the same way," said Pete. "How do they stay in a line even while they are doing tricks?"

"They are following a leader," answered Grandpa. "They practice marching behind their leader. If he turns right, they will also turn right. If he stops, they will also stop."

"It seems like that would take a lot of practice," said Pete.

"Yes," Grandpa said, "and look what happens after all of the practices."

Pete said, "Our Sunday school teacher said that God's Son Jesus was a great leader. She says it is important to follow Jesus and do what He says in the Bible."

"It is very important to follow Jesus," said Grandpa. "It takes lots of practice to be like Jesus."

"Just like it takes practice to be in a band?" asked Pete.

"Yes, just like the band. When we follow Jesus, we become like Him," said Grandpa.

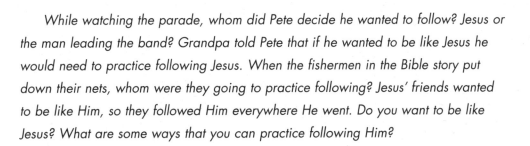

"I'm going to practice following Jesus," said Pete. "When I grow up, I want to be just like Him!"

"Me too," said Grandpa.

While watching the parade, whom did Pete decide he wanted to follow? Jesus or the man leading the band? Grandpa told Pete that if he wanted to be like Jesus he would need to practice following Jesus. When the fishermen in the Bible story put down their nets, whom were they going to practice following? Jesus' friends wanted to be like Him, so they followed Him everywhere He went. Do you want to be like Jesus? What are some ways that you can practice following Him?

STORY BOOSTERS

★ Adopt a missionary family as pen pals for your family. Talk about the ways that family has chosen to follow Jesus. Encourage YOUR family in any ways they are following Jesus like the disciples and your missionary friends.

★ Play a game that has your kids imitating actions that you do. As you play the game, review the story that tells how Jesus' disciples dropped what they were doing to follow Him.

STORMS

Daddy I'm feeling frightened
Daddy I'm feeling sad
All you have to do is call out to Jesus
Daddy I'm feeling lonely
Daddy I'm feeling hurt
All you have to do is call out to Jesus

Chorus:
Because Jesus will calm the storm in your life
No matter how the strong winds blow
No matter how the waters rage
Trust in Jesus and He will give you peace

In a boat on a lake
Jesus was calmly resting
The disciples were so scared; the rain was pouring
They screamed save us Lord
Jesus said don't you trust me
And with His mighty voice He calmed the storm

Chorus:
Jesus will calm the storms in our lives
No matter how the strong winds blow
No matter how the waters rage
Trust in Jesus and He will give us peace

Jesus will give you peace
Jesus will give you peace
May the peace of Jesus go with you forever

A PEACEFUL CHOICE

Maggie sat on her bed, hiding under the soft quilt her Grandma had made. Every time Maggie poked her head out from under the quilt, there was a loud crash and a bright flash that sent her right back into hiding. It was storming and Maggie was afraid. She looked out the window. Was the storm ever going to stop? Maggie didn't want to spend the rest of the day hiding on her bed.

She looked around her room for something to do that would keep her from thinking so much about the storm. Nothing sounded good to her.

Then she saw her Bible lying on her dresser. Her parents had given her the Bible for Christmas. She took her Bible to church every Sunday and read it at devotion time with her parents.

She picked up her Bible and looked through the pages. There were lots of colorful pictures. She remembered stories about Jesus and how

He helped people—even when they were afraid. As Maggie looked through her Bible and thought about Jesus, she realized that she wasn't afraid anymore. Then she read more stories about Jesus. Maggie liked reading her Bible.

Maggie heard her mom call from the kitchen. "Maggie, come and help set the table for dinner," her mom said.

Maggie closed the Bible and put it back on her dresser. Then Maggie prayed, "Thank You, Jesus, for the Bible so that I can read about You. And thank You for helping me not to be afraid of the storm."

Have you ever been afraid like Maggie was afraid? What did you do? The Bible tells about a time when Jesus' friends were afraid in a storm. Do you know what they did? They called on Jesus and He helped them by calming the storm. "He . . . said to the waves, 'Quiet! Be still!' Then the wind died down and it was completely calm" (Mark 4:39). The next time you are afraid, remember to go to Jesus and He will bring you peace.

STORY BOOSTERS

★ Enjoy making blue gelatin with your child according to the package. As it begins to set, add some gummy fish. Talk about the Bible story as you eat the "lake." What might the lake have been like during the storm? After the storm?

★ Talk with your child about situations in which she has found herself afraid. How did she react? Remind her that Jesus is our source of peace when we feel afraid. Pray together about something she is fearing right now.

THE NEWS

Chorus:
Did you hear the news about what Jesus did
He fed 5,000 people with some fish and some bread
Did you hear the news about what Jesus did

Well Jesus was talking to a crowd
About 5,000 and they were very loud
They were getting hungry and they wanted to eat
But they didn't know that Jesus would treat

The disciples said what are we gonna do
Jesus said God we're gonna leave it to You
He took some bread and a couple of fish
And turned it into a tasty dish

(Repeat chorus)

Because Jesus asked God to provide
His request was not denied
And just when you thought it was impossible
Everyone ate 'til their bellies were full

Some thought that it was unbelievable
That Jesus could do this miracle
So go run along and tell all your friends
Jesus fed 5,000 with some fish and bread

(Repeat chorus)

65

BILLY'S NEW HOME

Billy's family was moving to a new town. Billy's dad was going to be the minister at a different church. Billy was scared. His mom and dad said, "Billy, I know you don't really want to move, but God wants to use us in a new town. He will make sure we have everything we need; it will be OK."

When Billy visited his new school, he saw long halls filled with new faces. He saw large classrooms. The cafeteria seemed really scary when all the students came in. No one talked to Billy. Everyone already had friends. Billy wanted to cry. He wanted to go back to his old school.

Then Billy remembered what his mom said. He knew God would take care of him. He looked back down the hall and saw pretty pictures hanging on the walls. He looked in the classrooms and saw fun toys and lots of cool things to do. He walked back to the cafeteria. He saw one boy sitting alone.

"What's your name?" Billy asked.

"Michael," the boy replied.

"I'm Billy. I just moved and this is my new school," Billy said happily.

"Oh, cool," exclaimed Michael. "I have been praying for a new friend."

Billy went home, excited to tell his parents about his day at  school. "You were right! God made sure I had everything I needed—a great new school with lots of cool things to do AND a great new friend!"

God knew that Billy was going to need a new friend at his new school, so He took care of him. In the Bible we learn about a time when a big crowd of people Jesus was talking to became hungry. A young boy in the crowd had the only food— five pieces of bread and two fish. How did Jesus use that small lunch to take care of that big crowd? God will make sure you have everything you need, too, just like He took care of feeding the crowd with the boy's small lunch.

STORY BOOSTERS

★ Help your child to identify the basic needs of life—food, clothing, water, a place to live—as opposed to the things he wants—games, toys, a new computer. Then review the Bible story and talk about why Jesus fed the people.

★ Take your child grocery shopping with you. Allow him to choose a different food that you don't normally buy. Talk about how God provides for all our needs—He even gives us choices! Thank God for good food to eat.

DON'T SHOO THEM AWAY

Once there were some mothers
Who brought their children to Jesus
They asked Him to bless their little ones
Because they knew that He was God's Son
Then there were the disciples
Who normally were pretty nice
They said to the kids don't bother Him
He's got better things to do
And Jesus said, that's not what you should do

Chorus:
Shoo, shoo, shoo don't shoo them away
Shoo, shoo, shoo don't shoo them away
For the kingdom of God belongs to them this day

Jesus said this I tell you
We've got to be like little ones
And come to God with an open heart
Because we're all God's children
Then He hugged them gently
And placed His hands on their heads
I bless you in the name of God
And the children were blessed
And that is why Jesus said

(Repeat chorus twice)

Shoo, shoo, shoo don't shoo them away (10 times)
For the kingdom of God belongs to them this day

SPENCER'S FRIEND

Spencer had a problem. He didn't know what to do about the boys who teased him at school. He really needed to talk to someone.

"Hey, Mom," Spencer started.

"In a minute, Honey, I'm busy right now," said Mom. Spencer went to find Dad.

"Dad, can I talk to you for a minute?" he asked.

"Sure. But I need to clean up and get to a meeting. Can you tell me later?" Dad hurried to his bedroom.

"All I want is someone to talk to!" Spencer said as he plopped down on the couch. He felt lonely. He looked out the front window. He began to think about what his Sunday school teacher had told them. They had talked about how much Jesus loves children. One time Jesus let children come to Him, even though His helpers said no.

Spencer realized that Jesus loved him too. Jesus would listen to him. So Spencer prayed, "Dear Jesus, please help me find a way to get along with the boys at school."

When he finished praying, he felt better. It felt good to tell someone about his problem. He walked into the kitchen. Mom was doing dishes. "What did you need, Spencer?"

Spencer sat down at the table and told his mom all about the boys at school. Then he told his mom about praying for help. He was glad that Jesus loved him and wanted to listen.

In Mark 10:14 Jesus says, "Let the little children come to me." What children is Jesus talking about? Do you think Jesus wants you to come to Him? Sure He does! He wants you to come to Him because He loves you and He wants to be your friend. So, the next time you feel lonely like Spencer did, remember that Jesus loves you and He will listen to anything you want to tell Him.

STORY BOOSTERS

★ Tell the story of Jesus and the children by giving each family member a different role—disciples, children, Jesus. Then talk about how each of the characters may have felt. Pray together, thanking Jesus for His love.

★ Talk with your child about love and acceptance. Ask if she knows someone who isn't accepted by others. Invite that child over for dinner to show love and acceptance of the children as Jesus did.

A FRIEND INDEED

A man went walkin' on a sunny day
Lookin' at the scenery along the way
Suddenly he heard a voice behind him say
Let me have your wallet 'cuz it's time to pay

Then those crooks all gathered around
The man cried for help but there was none to be found
The bad guys knocked him to the ground
And when they were through he couldn't make a sound

Chorus:
The robbers left him lying there in the sand
Along came a stranger from a foreign land
He saw the man needed a helping hand and said
A friend in need is a friend indeed

A priest walked by and could've helped for sure
But he was too busy so he closed the door
The temple worker had to go mop the floor
Why don't people help each other anymore

Jesus said my neighbor is a person in need
A kind and helpful person is what I should be
If everyone was helpful you can plainly see
The world would be better; wouldn't you agree

(Repeat chorus)

The stranger knew that he could show the love
 of the Lord
He paid the doctor's bill as much as he could afford
The doctor let the man stay until his health was restored
Because a friend in need is a friend indeed (3 times)

FLOWERS OF FRIENDSHIP

Naomi and Mom were on their way to visit Grandma. They stopped by the flower shop where Naomi picked out some beautiful flowers to brighten Grandma's day. She lived in a care center with lots of other grandmas and grandpas. Grandma always had a smile for Naomi. But Grandma's friend, Mrs. Thomas, never smiled. She mostly just stared out the window. Naomi wished that she could do something to help Mrs. Thomas.

I have a great idea! Naomi said to herself. Naomi told her mom and she thought it was a great idea too!

Soon they were back in the car and headed for the care center. Naomi was so excited she couldn't stop grinning! She grinned all the way down the hall to Grandma's room.

"Hi, Grandma," she said, putting some flowers in Grandma's hand.

Naomi walked to the other side of the room and gently touched Mrs. Thomas's hand. Mrs. Thomas turned her head. Naomi held out a second bunch of flowers.

"Excuse me," said Naomi. "I brought these for you." Tears gathered in Mrs. Thomas's eyes.

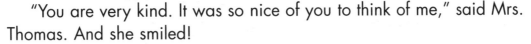

"Thank you," said Mrs. Thomas. "But I can't get up to give them water. Maybe you should give them to your grandma instead."

"Don't worry. I'll put them in water. These are for YOU!" Naomi said excitedly. She hoped the flowers would make Mrs. Thomas happy.

"You are very kind. It was so nice of you to think of me," said Mrs. Thomas. And she smiled!

In the Bible story about the Samaritan man, Jesus tells us, "Love your neighbor as yourself" (Luke 10:27). What does Jesus mean? He wants us to treat everyone with love—even the people we DON'T know! Naomi showed love to her neighbor, Mrs. Thomas, by giving her flowers. How did the man from a foreign land show love to his neighbor in the Bible story song? What can you do to show love to someone by being a helper?

STORY BOOSTERS

★ Read the Bible story from Luke 10:25-37 together. Choose a family project to put into practice what Jesus taught. Try having each family member gather some clothes to give to a family in need.

★ Let your child help to make a simple meal to share with someone you know who is sick. Recall the words of Jesus as you prepare to deliver the meal. Then deliver it as a family.

AND THERE WERE 10

From far away
Ten lepers yelled to the Lord please heal us
He looked up and said without a fuss
Go to the priests and show them you are healed

So then they went
They noticed that their skin was getting well
They started feeling oh so swell
Then nine of them went on to live their lives

Chorus:
And there were 10
But only one came back to thank the Lord
Only one came back to give Him praise, uh-huh
He knelt right down at Jesus' feet
To thank Him for a love so sweet
And show us just exactly what to do

So now we know
To thank the Lord for the things He gives to us
Mercy love forgiveness
And remember that all good things come from Him

Ending chorus:
Just like the one
He was the only one who came back to the Lord
The only one to give Him praise, uh-huh
He knelt right down at Jesus' feet
To thank Him for a love so sweet
And show us just exactly what to do

THE PLAYFUL PUPPY

Every time Shelly and her parents went to town, she asked to go to the pet store. Shelly loved to play with the puppies.

On her way home from school one day, Shelly heard something prancing along behind her on the sidewalk. When she turned around, there was a snuggly little brown and white puppy! It followed her all the way home. Shelly hoped with all her might that Mom and Dad would let her keep him.

When Mom saw the puppy, she looked worried. "Shelly, this puppy belongs to someone," she said. "He is wearing a collar."

Shelly was disappointed, but she knew they needed to find the puppy's owner. Dad started calling some of their neighbors and found that the puppy belonged to Mr. Price. He lived down at the other end of the street. "I'll be over after dinner," Shelly heard her dad say.

Shelly was sad. She didn't want the puppy to leave. Her dad tried to make her feel better by saying, "Maybe you can get a puppy of your own soon. Shelly did feel a little better. Still, she really liked *that* puppy.

After dinner, Dad took the snuggly little brown and white puppy home.

It only took a minute, but when Dad came back, he was carrying something under his arm.

"The puppy!" cried Shelly, as she ran to give the snuggly puppy a hug.

"Mr. Price's dog had six puppies," her dad said. "He wanted you to have one as a reward."

Although she was excited to play with her new puppy, Shelly knew there was something else she had to do first. She ran in to call Mr. Price. She wanted to thank him for giving her the snuggly little brown and white puppy.

Shelly remembered to thank the man who gave her the puppy. In the Bible story, Jesus healed 10 men who were sick with leprosy. How many of the men remembered to thank Jesus for what He had done? How many of the men were so excited about being healed that they forgot to thank Jesus? Who do you want to be like? The nine men who forgot to thank Jesus or the one man who remembered to thank Him?

STORY BOOSTERS

★ Make a list together of 10 things for which you don't always remember to thank God. As prayer times roll around over the next week, use the list to help you remember to be thankful.

★ When your child remembers to thank you for something you did, reward him with a favorite treat. As you do, recall together the story about the one man with leprosy who said, "Thanks!"

ZACCHAEUS

Zacchaeus was a little man, a wee little man
He lied a lot and cheated everyone in the land
That's why no one liked him and the sight of him they couldn't stand

Then one day Jesus came to visit his town
Zacchaeus went to hear the greatest teacher around
But he was too short to see a thing from where he was on the ground

Then he started climbing up a sycamore tree
He was so excited he could finally see
When he looked at Jesus he heard a strange sound
Zacchaeus won't you come back down

Jesus said, I want to come and visit your home
And Jesus showed him kindness that he never had known
Zacchaeus gave back all the money that he kept for his own

God can take a person who is selfish and rude
And turn him into someone with a new attitude
Jesus was a friend to Zacchaeus in the tree
And Jesus is a friend to me

God can take a person who is selfish and rude
And turn him into someone with a new attitude
Jesus was a friend to Zacchaeus in the tree
And Jesus is a friend to me
Jesus is a friend to me (twice)

A NEW FRIEND

It was almost time for the lunch bell to ring. Ria, Beth, and two of their friends always sat together at lunch. They sat at a table by themselves. Ria put her head near Beth's. "Hurry when the bell rings. We need to make sure we get our seats," she whispered.

"Why?" asked Beth out loud.

"The new girl, Sami, might try to sit at our table. We need to make sure we get there first." Ria whispered louder this time.

"Why?" asked Beth.

"She's new. We have always sat together at lunch. We don't want to add anyone new," Ria said.

"Oh," said Beth, with a funny look on her face.

The lunch bell rang. Ria and the other girls grabbed their lunches and hurried to a table in a corner of the lunchroom. Beth took her lunch and walked straight over to Sami's desk.

"Can I eat with you today?" she asked. Sami looked up in surprise, but nodded. The two girls talked all the way to the lunchroom.

"My mom put an extra cookie in my lunch. Do you want one?" asked Beth.

"Sure," said Sami. "Thanks."

"Are you coming, Beth?" called Ria.

"No," she answered. "I'm eating with Sami today."

Ria shrugged and made a face at Beth. But Beth didn't care. Sami's smile was worth it. Beth was glad she had been nice to Sami.

Beth did something that Jesus would do by being a friend to Sami when the other girls didn't want to. The Bible tells about a man named Zacchaeus. He was a man with whom no one wanted to be friends. But along came Jesus, and what did Jesus do? He went to Zacchaeus's house! Do you know someone who could use a new friend? Invite your new friend to come over and play with you!

STORY BOOSTERS

★ Pick a familiar tune such as "Are You Sleeping?" and have your child come up with his own lyrics about being a friend. Don't forget to include ways that Jesus is our friend!

★ Gather some beads and bead string. Enjoy making bead jewelry together with your child. As you do, talk about ways you can thank Jesus for being a friend. Share the jewelry with a friend, or wear it as a reminder of Jesus' friendship.

ALIVE!

Jesus was at the olive trees
Oh, oh, please tell us
But Judas brought the Pharisees
Why did they make a fuss
Because Jesus said He, He was the Messiah

They arrested Him and beat Him down
Why did they do these things
And made Him wear a thorny crown
Wasn't He the King of kings
And they nailed Him up high, high, high on the cross
But three days later He rose again

Chorus:
Praise the Lord; Jesus is alive
(Repeat 3 times)

Mary cried all through the night
Poor Mary, why'd she cry
She thought that her Savior died
Poor Mary, didn't know why
She thought Jesus was gone, gone, gone, gone for good

Then two angels said to her
Oh tell me what'd they say
Why do you look so hurt
The stone was rolled away
Now you don't have to cry, cry, cry anymore
And then she saw the risen Lord

(Repeat chorus)

God sent His Son to die for the world
For every man and woman, boy and girl
His death was surely not the end
And three days later He rose again
Praise the Lord; Jesus is alive

(Repeat chorus)

THE EASTER PLAY

Becky was so happy! The church was having an Easter play and Kim was going with Becky and her family. Kim's family didn't go to church. Becky was glad that Kim would learn about Jesus when she came to the play.

The play began. Jesus was walking with His followers when they saw a man who was blind. Jesus stopped and healed the man. The man who was blind could now see!

It was a miracle! Jesus did many miracles and many people loved Jesus. But some people hated Jesus. They didn't like Jesus because He did miracles.

The mean people who hated Jesus had Him killed on a cross. Jesus' followers all went home very sad.

Jesus was buried in a tomb. On Sunday morning, a woman named Mary went to the tomb. The stone in front of the tomb had been moved.

Mary ran and told some of Jesus' followers what she had seen. The followers were sad, but they went with Mary back to the tomb.

Mary saw two angels. They told Mary, "Jesus is alive!"

When the play was over, Kim said, "That story was sad, but it had a happy ending. Becky, I'm really glad that Jesus is alive, but why did Jesus have to die?"

Becky's dad overheard the girls talking. He began to tell them more about Jesus and how much God loves them.

"God so loved the world that he gave his one and only Son, that whoever believes in him shall . . . have eternal life" (John 3:16, 17). Jesus died and lives again so that our sins will be forgiven and we can live forever with God! How does that make you feel? It made Becky feel so happy that she wanted to share the story with her friend Kim. In the Bible story, when Mary found out that Jesus was alive, she was so happy she ran to tell all of Jesus' friends!

STORY BOOSTERS

★ Prepare resurrection baskets for some elderly neighbors. Include cross-shaped cookies, votive candles, spring candies, and artificial flowers. Help your child write a note telling how happy she is that Jesus is alive!

★ Talk with your child about what sin is and what it means to be forgiven. Pray together, thanking God that Jesus is alive and our sins are forgiven.

DYNAMIC DUO

Chorus:
Let's give it up for the dynamic duo
They are the heroes of the book of Acts
Paul and Silas are on my list of heroes in this world
Let's give it up for the dynamic duo

They didn't have any super weapons or fancy cars
They just had faith and that got them locked behind bars
They didn't wear capes and they didn't fly
So why are they heroes
I'll tell you why
Paul and Silas traveled far telling the world about Jesus

(Repeat chorus)

They were preaching in Philippi and they were thrown in prison
They were singing about Jesus; the guard hated to listen
But then an earthquake made the jail shake
The doors opened but nobody escaped
The guard got down on his knees and said
I want to know this Jesus
That's why Paul and Silas were heroes

(Repeat chorus)

JESSICA

Jessica sat next to Tomika on the bus. "Can you come over to play this weekend?" asked Jessica.

"That would be fun," said Tomika.

"I'm going to my aunt's house tomorrow," Jessica said. "But you could come over on Sunday to play."

"My family goes to church on Sunday," said Tomika.

"You have to go to church every Sunday? How boring!" said Jessica.

Tomika didn't answer. She felt bad. Why hadn't she told Jessica that church wasn't boring? Tomika always had lots of fun at church. She loved to learn about Jesus.

All weekend, Tomika planned what she could say to Jessica. On Monday morning when Jessica got on the bus, Tomika said, "I'm sorry we couldn't play this weekend. Maybe next Saturday you could spend the night at my house. Then you could come with me to church on Sunday."

Jessica was very quiet. She wasn't sure she wanted to do that.

"We'll have lots of fun!" Tomika added. "At church we learn about my very best friend, Jesus!"

"Jesus is your best friend? Why?" Jessica asked.

Tomika responded, "Because He is God's Son. Jesus loves me so much that He died on a cross for me."

Jessica thought about that. She said, "I will ask my mom if I can spend the night at your house. Can you tell me more about your friend Jesus now? Or do I have to wait to hear about Him at church?"

Tomika smiled. Then she told Jessica about how much she loved Jesus.

In the story we just read, what did Tomika do when she remembered how much fun she had at church? She wanted to share her fun and her friend Jesus with Jessica. The Bible tells a story about a time when Paul and Silas were in jail. They loved Jesus so much, they sang to Him and told others about Him even when they were in jail! Have you ever told your friends about the fun you have at church or about how much you love Jesus?

STORY BOOSTERS

★ Make some jail bar treats. Spread white icing on graham crackers. Then apply jail bars using a tube of gel icing. Recall the story of Paul and Silas. Ask God to help you be brave and tell others about Jesus.

★ Use chains of paper loops to put around your child's hands and feet. Talk about the Bible story in which Paul and Silas were confined. Talk about ways to tell others about Jesus while confined like Paul.

INDEX OF CONTEMPORARY STORIES

INDEX OF SONGS

Welcome to the Family!

Heritage Builders®

Helping You Build a Family of Faith

We hope you've enjoyed this book. Heritage Builders was founded in 1995 by three fathers with a passion for the next generation. As a new ministry of Focus on the Family, Heritage Builders strives to equip, train, and motivate parents to become intentional about building a strong spiritual heritage.

It's quite a challenge for busy parents to find ways to build a spiritual foundation for their families—especially in a way they enjoy and understand. Through activities and participation, children can learn biblical truth in a way they can understand, enjoy—and *remember.*

Passing along a heritage of Christian faith to your family is a parent's highest calling. Heritage Builders' goal is to encourage and empower you in this great mission with practical resources and inspiring ideas that really work—and help your children develop a lasting love for God.

* * *

How To Reach Us

For more information, visit our Heritage Builders Web site! Log on to
www.heritagebuilders.com to discover new resources, sample activities, and ideas to
help you pass on a spiritual heritage. To request any of these resources, simply call Focus on the
Family at 1-800-A-FAMILY (1-800-232-6459) or in Canada, call 1-800-661-9800.
Or send your request to Focus on the Family, Colorado Springs, CO 80995.
In Canada, write Focus on the Family, P.O. Box 9800, Stn. Terminal, Vancouver, B.C. V6B 4G3

To learn more about Focus on the Family or to find out if there is an associate
office in your country, please visit www.family.org.

We'd love to hear from you!